SAMSUNG GALAXY S25
ULTRA USER GUIDE

Optimizing Performance with Advanced Features and Tools

AARON P. BONNER

COPYRIGHT

TABLE OF CONTENTS

INTRODUCTION

Welcome to the Samsung Galaxy S25 Ultra User Guide—your ultimate resource for mastering one of the most powerful smartphones ever created. The Samsung Galaxy S25 Ultra represents the pinnacle of technological innovation, designed to meet the demands of today's tech-savvy users. Whether you're a professional, a content creator, or someone who simply wants the best mobile experience, this device is built to deliver extraordinary performance, exceptional camera quality, and a range of features that will enhance your daily life.

In this guide, we will take you through every essential aspect of your new Galaxy S25 Ultra, from setting up your device to unlocking its advanced capabilities. This book will help you get the most out of your phone by guiding you step-by-step on how to use, customize, and troubleshoot your device. With the Galaxy S25 Ultra, you can expect more than just a smartphone—expect a powerful tool that enhances your productivity, creativity, and entertainment.

So, whether you are just getting started or want to explore some of the advanced features, let's dive into the world of the Samsung Galaxy S25 Ultra and explore the incredible possibilities that await.

Unpacking the Samsung Galaxy S25 Ultra

The first step in truly understanding your Samsung Galaxy S25 Ultra is to explore its design and contents. The moment you unbox your device, you're greeted with an impressive display, elegant design, and the promise of cutting-edge technology. But what's inside the box? Let's take a closer look.

What's in the Box?

When you first open the box, you'll find:

Samsung Galaxy S25 Ultra: The star of the show, boasting a 6.9-inch Dynamic AMOLED 2X display, a 200MP camera system, and cutting-edge AI features.

USB-C Charging Cable: For fast charging and data transfer.

SIM Ejector Tool: Essential for inserting or removing your SIM card.

Quick Start Guide: Provides a brief overview to help you get started quickly.

Warranty Information and Safety Guide: Important details about your device's warranty and safety measures.

With these items in hand, you're ready to embark on your journey to master the Samsung Galaxy S25 Ultra.

Setting Up Your Galaxy S25 Ultra

Getting Started with the Basics

The setup process of the Galaxy S25 Ultra is intuitive and simple. After powering on the device, you'll be prompted to select your language, connect to a Wi-Fi network, and log in to your Samsung account. If you're upgrading from an older device, transferring your apps, contacts, and settings is a breeze with Samsung's Smart Switch.

Once set up, you can personalize your device by adding widgets, adjusting the wallpaper, and organizing your home screen. This user-friendly interface, combined with One UI—Samsung's custom skin built on Android—ensures that your experience is both intuitive and enjoyable.

Security First: Setting Up Your Fingerprint and Face Recognition

To keep your data safe and secure, the Galaxy S25 Ultra offers biometric authentication features. You can set up fingerprint recognition and facial recognition for added convenience and security. These features provide seamless access to your phone while ensuring that your personal information stays protected.

Fingerprint Setup: Simply place your finger on the screen to register your fingerprint. This allows you to unlock your phone, authorize payments, and more with just a touch.

Face Recognition: By using the front camera to scan your face, you can unlock your phone with a glance, making it both secure and convenient.

The Galaxy S25 Ultra Display: A Visual Masterpiece

One of the most striking features of the Galaxy S25 Ultra is its display. The device boasts a 6.9-inch Dynamic AMOLED 2X display, offering brilliant colors, deep blacks, and true-to-life images. Whether you're watching videos, playing games, or browsing through photos, the S25 Ultra's display is engineered to provide a superior viewing experience.

Immersive Viewing

With a resolution of 3200 x 1440 pixels and a 120Hz refresh rate, the Galaxy S25 Ultra delivers stunning visuals that are smooth and detailed. The high refresh rate ensures that every interaction on the screen feels fluid, whether you're scrolling through social media or playing action-packed games.

Adaptive Display: Tailoring to Your Needs

Thanks to its adaptive display technology, the Galaxy S25 Ultra automatically adjusts the screen's brightness and color balance depending on the environment and content being displayed. Whether you're indoors or outside, the screen optimizes for comfort and clarity.

Exploring the Camera System: A Photography Revolution

The Samsung Galaxy S25 Ultra introduces one of the most powerful camera systems ever seen in a smartphone. With a 200MP main sensor, 10MP telephoto lens, 12MP ultrawide lens, and 10MP periscope lens with 10x optical zoom, the camera setup on the S25 Ultra is designed to deliver professional-level photography.

Capturing Details with Precision

The 200MP camera allows you to take ultra-high-definition photos with incredible clarity. Whether you're shooting landscapes, portraits, or macro shots, the level of detail captured is unmatched. For those who love zooming in, the

10x optical zoom ensures that distant subjects remain crisp and clear.

AI-Powered Photography Features

Samsung has integrated AI to enhance the photographic experience. Scene Optimizer detects and adjusts settings based on what you're photographing, ensuring that your images always look their best. Additionally, Super Steady Video makes sure your video footage remains stable, even during movement.

Night Mode: Excellent Low-Light Performance

Night photography has never been easier. With the Galaxy S25 Ultra's Night Mode, you can capture incredible photos in low-light conditions, with enhanced detail and less noise. Whether it's a candlelit dinner or a night out, the camera adjusts to deliver clear, bright images.

Performance: Speed and Power in Your Hands

Under the hood, the Samsung Galaxy S25 Ultra is powered by the Qualcomm Snapdragon 8 Gen 3 processor, making it one of the most powerful smartphones available today. Paired with 12GB or 16GB of RAM, this phone handles everything from intensive gaming sessions to multitasking with ease.

Optimized for Speed and Efficiency

The device runs on the Android 14 operating system with One UI 6, providing a clean and efficient user interface that's both fast and responsive. Apps open instantly, and tasks are performed without a hitch, ensuring that your device can keep up with your fast-paced life.

Gaming and Multimedia: A Performance Beast

For those who love gaming or consuming media on the go, the Galaxy S25 Ultra is equipped with a 120Hz display, stereo speakers, and enhanced GPU performance, making it the ideal device for gaming, watching movies, or streaming content.

Battery Life and Charging: Keep Going All Day

The Galaxy S25 Ultra is equipped with a 5000mAh battery, designed to last all day with normal use. But what makes the battery even better is its ability to charge quickly and wirelessly.

Fast Charging and Wireless PowerShare

With 45W fast charging, you can charge your device to 50% in just 30 minutes. Need to share your charge with another device? Use the Wireless PowerShare feature to charge other phones, earbuds, or wearables wirelessly.

Advanced Features: Unlock the Full Potential

Samsung DeX: Desktop Experience in Your Pocket

With Samsung DeX, your Galaxy S25 Ultra can transform into a desktop PC. Simply connect it to a monitor, keyboard, and mouse to enjoy a full desktop experience, making it ideal for work, presentations, or even gaming on a larger screen.

Multi-Window and App Pairing: Enhanced Productivity

The Galaxy S25 Ultra's Multi-Window Mode allows you to run two apps at the same time. App Pairing lets you open your favorite apps with just one tap—perfect for multitaskers who need to keep work and play at their fingertips.

Security and Privacy: Keeping Your Data Safe

The Samsung Galaxy S25 Ultra offers a range of security features to ensure that your personal data remains safe and private.

Samsung Knox: Military-Grade Security

Samsung Knox provides military-grade security to protect your device from malware, hackers, and other security threats. It offers encryption and real-time protection to keep your sensitive data safe.

Secure Folder: Storing Your Private Information

With Secure Folder, you can keep your personal files, apps, and photos separate from the rest of your data. Lock them with a password, fingerprint, or PIN, ensuring that no one else can access them.

Your Journey with the Galaxy S25 Ultra Begins

The Samsung Galaxy S25 Ultra is not just a smartphone—it's a statement of what technology can do for your life. From stunning photography and powerful performance to innovative features like Samsung DeX and the S Pen, this device has been built to elevate your everyday experiences.

With the knowledge gained from this user guide, you are now equipped to get the most out of your Galaxy S25 Ultra. Whether you are a photography enthusiast, a productivity powerhouse, or a digital content creator, the S25 Ultra is designed to meet your needs, while providing you with a premium experience every time you pick it up.

It's time to unleash the full potential of your Samsung Galaxy S25 Ultra—explore, create, and innovate with one of the most advanced smartphones on the market today.

CHAPTER 1

Getting Started with Your Samsung Galaxy S25 Ultra

Congratulations on your new Samsung Galaxy S25 Ultra! Whether you're upgrading from a previous device or this is your first Samsung phone, the S25 Ultra is designed to provide a premium experience. In this chapter, we'll walk you through the initial steps to get your device up and running, and help you make the most out of the features available right from the start. Let's dive into unboxing your phone, powering it up, and setting up the essential features that will allow you to get the best experience.

Unboxing and First Impressions

What's Included in the Box

When you open the box of your Samsung Galaxy S25 Ultra, you're presented with everything you need to get started. The packaging is sleek, and the presentation matches the quality of the device itself. Here's a rundown of what you'll find inside:

Samsung Galaxy S25 Ultra: The star of the show, this is the centerpiece of the box. The device comes in a protective plastic wrap, with its stunning 6.9-inch Dynamic AMOLED 2X display covered by a pre-installed screen protector to protect it from scratches during shipping.

USB-C Charging Cable: A fast-charging cable that connects to your device's USB-C port, ensuring a quick and efficient charge. The cable supports 45W fast charging for super-fast battery replenishment.

SIM Ejector Tool: This tool is used to remove the SIM tray from the device so you can insert or replace your SIM card. It's a small, yet essential tool that allows you to use cellular data and make calls.

Quick Start Guide: A helpful guide that walks you through the basics of setting up your phone, offering a high-level overview of essential functions. This guide also includes safety instructions and warranty information.

Warranty and Safety Information: These documents outline the terms of your warranty and provide important safety precautions and guidelines for the device.

Now that you've unboxed your phone, let's take a closer look at its design and first impressions.

Design Overview: First Look at the Build Quality and Display

The Samsung Galaxy S25 Ultra has been meticulously designed to provide both functionality and elegance. From its solid build to its stunning display, the S25 Ultra sets a new standard for what a flagship smartphone should look and feel like.

Build Quality: The device feels premium in the hand, thanks to the combination of metallic edges and glass that's smooth yet resistant to fingerprints. The phone has a robust feel, with an overall weight that communicates its high-end construction without being cumbersome. The back is made of Gorilla Glass Victus 2, which ensures durability, scratch resistance, and impact resistance.

Display: The 6.9-inch Dynamic AMOLED 2X display is an absolute showstopper. Offering a 3200 x 1440 resolution, it boasts 120Hz adaptive refresh rate, making scrolling buttery smooth and gaming incredibly immersive. The colors are vibrant, with deep blacks and vivid details, thanks to HDR10+ support. Whether you're watching videos, browsing photos, or reading text, the S25 Ultra's display makes everything look stunning.

Physical Buttons and Ports: On the right side of the phone, you'll find the volume rockers and the power button. The power button doubles as the Bixby button, enabling easy access to Samsung's voice assistant. The SIM card tray is on the left side of the device, and the USB-C charging port is located at the bottom, flanked by the speaker grille and microphone. At the top, you'll find a secondary microphone for noise cancellation. The S Pen slot is also positioned conveniently on the bottom edge, allowing easy access to the stylus.

Now that you have a feel for the device's design, it's time to turn it on and begin the setup process.

Powering Up and Initial Setup

Turning On Your Device for the First Time

Turning on your Samsung Galaxy S25 Ultra for the first time is simple. Here's how to do it:

Press and hold the power button (on the right side) for a few seconds until the Samsung logo appears on the screen.

The phone will vibrate slightly, and you will be greeted with the initial setup screen.

Connecting to Wi-Fi and Setting Up Your Samsung Account

Once your phone powers up, the first step is to connect to a Wi-Fi network. This will ensure that your device can download necessary updates, apps, and sync your data. Here's how:

Choose your language and region: Select your preferred language and set your region, which will help optimize your device for the correct time zone and settings.

Connect to Wi-Fi: Choose your home Wi-Fi network from the list and enter the password to establish the connection. If you don't have access to Wi-Fi, you can proceed by using mobile data.

Sign in to your Samsung account: You'll be prompted to log in to your Samsung account. This account allows you to access various Samsung services, such as Samsung Cloud, Samsung Pay, and Samsung Health. If you don't have an account, you can create one at this step.

Once connected to Wi-Fi and logged into your Samsung account, the device will check for software updates and make sure everything is up-to-date.

Restoring Data from Your Old Device

If you are upgrading from another Samsung device or a different Android phone, you can restore your data seamlessly using Samsung Smart Switch. This tool makes it easy to transfer your contacts, messages, photos, apps, and more from your old device to your new Galaxy S25 Ultra.

Smart Switch will detect your previous device and allow you to transfer data either wirelessly or via a USB cable.

If you're switching from an iPhone, Smart Switch can also transfer data from iCloud, such as contacts, photos, and calendar events.

Once your data is restored, you're ready to move on to the final steps of setting up your device.

Setting Up Your Preferred Language and Region

After connecting to Wi-Fi and logging into your Samsung account, you'll have the option to select your preferred language and region. This setting will affect everything from text language to time and date formats. For example, if you prefer using English (United States), selecting this will ensure that your phone displays the correct language, time zone, and default regional settings.

You can also customize your keyboard settings, including the keyboard layout (e.g., QWERTY) and language preferences for easier typing.

Setting Up Your Fingerprint and Face Recognition

The Samsung Galaxy S25 Ultra comes equipped with biometric security options to help keep your device safe while ensuring quick and easy access. You can set up fingerprint recognition and facial recognition for an added layer of protection.

How to Configure Your Fingerprint for Security

The in-display fingerprint scanner on the Galaxy S25 Ultra provides a convenient and secure way to unlock your device. Here's how to set it up:

Go to Settings > Biometrics and security > Fingerprints.

Select Add fingerprint. You will be prompted to place your finger on the display's fingerprint sensor. The phone will scan your fingerprint, asking you to adjust the positioning of your finger to get a full scan.

After the scan is complete, follow the on-screen instructions to finish the setup.

You can add multiple fingerprints for family members or different fingers for your own use.

Once set up, you can use your fingerprint to unlock your phone, authorize purchases, or access secure apps.

Enabling and Setting Up Facial Recognition

In addition to the fingerprint scanner, the Galaxy S25 Ultra also offers face recognition. This option allows you to unlock your device with just a glance. Here's how to set it up:

Go to Settings > Biometrics and security > Face recognition.

Tap on Register face and follow the prompts to scan your face. The device uses the front camera to analyze your facial features.

Once completed, you can use face unlock as an alternative method to access your device quickly and securely.

Benefits of Biometric Security

Both fingerprint recognition and face recognition offer several advantages:

Quick and Secure Access: These methods provide faster access than traditional PINs or passwords while keeping your device secure.

Convenience: You no longer need to remember a password or swipe gestures, making the phone unlocking process incredibly easy and intuitive.

Improved Privacy: Biometric data is stored securely and can be used for additional features like securing apps and making transactions with Samsung Pay.

These security features ensure that your Samsung Galaxy S25 Ultra is protected while maintaining ease of use. With Samsung Knox, you get a multi-layered defense system that adds another layer of security, keeping your sensitive data safe from potential threats.

Your Samsung Galaxy S25 Ultra Awaits

Congratulations, you've successfully set up your Samsung Galaxy S25 Ultra! By now, you've gone through the basics: unboxing, setting up your account, restoring data, and securing your phone with biometric authentication. You're ready to begin exploring the vast array of features this powerful device offers, from its cutting-edge camera system to its advanced performance capabilities.

As you continue using your Galaxy S25 Ultra, keep this guide handy to ensure you're maximizing all the device's features. Whether you're a tech enthusiast looking to dive deeper into customization, a professional relying on your phone for productivity, or a creative seeking to capture stunning photos and videos, the Galaxy S25 Ultra has something to offer.

Now that you've unlocked its core functionality, it's time to explore the advanced features and make the Galaxy S25 Ultra truly your own. Enjoy the incredible mobile experience that awaits you!

CHAPTER 2

Navigating the Galaxy S25 Ultra Interface

The Samsung Galaxy S25 Ultra is equipped with One UI, Samsung's custom Android skin, designed to give you an intuitive and seamless experience. Understanding how to navigate the interface is essential to unlock the full potential of your device. In this chapter, we will dive into the key aspects of using the Galaxy S25 Ultra, starting with the home screen and moving through to quick settings, notifications, and personalization options. Whether you're a new user or a seasoned Android enthusiast, this guide will help you make the most out of your Galaxy S25 Ultra.

The Home Screen: Understanding the Basics

Your home screen is the starting point for navigating your Galaxy S25 Ultra. It serves as the central hub where you can organize and access your apps, widgets, and shortcuts. Understanding the home screen layout and how to personalize it will help you get the most out of your device. Let's break down how you can organize and customize it to suit your needs.

Customizing Your Home Screen Layout

The home screen layout is one of the most flexible and customizable aspects of the Galaxy S25 Ultra. You can tweak everything from the number of app icons displayed to the arrangement of widgets. Here's how you can start customizing:

Adjusting the Grid Size:

To make more room for your apps, you can adjust the grid size on your home screen. Go to Settings > Display > Home screen and select the grid size option.

You can choose from a smaller grid to fit more apps or a larger one for easier access to apps with bigger icons.

Adding a New Home Screen Page:

If you want additional space to organize your apps or widgets, you can add more home screen pages. Simply tap and hold on an empty part of the home screen, and then drag the app icons or widgets onto a new page.

You can also drag the home screen dots at the bottom to reorder the pages, allowing you to customize how apps and widgets are grouped.

App Drawer and Home Screen Pages:

You can choose whether apps are shown directly on the home screen or if you want to keep them in the app drawer. This setting can be adjusted in Settings > Display > Home screen > Home screen layout. You can choose either "Apps only" to show apps in the drawer or "Apps and Home screen" to have both on the main page.

Adding Apps, Widgets, and Shortcuts

The Galaxy S25 Ultra offers many ways to add elements to your home screen for quick access to your most-used features. Here's how you can add apps, widgets, and shortcuts:

Adding Apps:

To add an app to the home screen, simply tap and hold the app icon from the app drawer and drag it to the desired location on the home screen.

You can also organize apps by folders. Just drag one app on top of another to create a folder and name it according to your preference (e.g., "Work," "Games").

Adding Widgets:

Widgets are small, interactive features that give you quick access to app functions or live information. To add a widget, long press on the home screen, then tap Widgets. You'll be able to scroll through a variety of available widgets, such as weather, calendar, clock, and news.

Once you've found a widget, drag it to the home screen and resize it to fit your layout preferences.

Adding Shortcuts:

Shortcuts are customizable actions within apps that allow quick access to specific features (e.g., calling a favorite contact or checking your calendar). To add a shortcut, tap and hold the app icon from the home screen, then select Create shortcut and choose the specific action.

Organizing Your App Drawer

Your app drawer is where all your installed apps live, and it's important to organize it in a way that makes sense to you. The Galaxy S25 Ultra allows for extensive customization:

Arranging Apps Alphabetically or by Category:

In the app drawer, tap the three vertical dots in the top-right corner and select Sort by. You can choose Alphabetical order or Custom order, allowing you to organize apps by category, such as productivity, games, or social media.

Creating Folders in the App Drawer:

Just like the home screen, you can create folders in the app drawer for better organization. Tap and hold an app and drag it onto another app to create a folder. You can name the folder and add multiple apps to it.

Search Function:

If you have many apps, the search bar at the top of the app drawer allows you to quickly find the app you're looking for. Just type in the app name and tap it to open.

Quick Settings and Notifications

The Quick Settings panel and notifications on your Galaxy S25 Ultra provide an efficient way to manage your device's settings and stay informed about what's happening. Let's break down how these features work and how you can customize them.

Understanding the Quick Settings Panel

The Quick Settings panel is a convenient place where you can access essential functions without needing to navigate through the settings menu. To access it, swipe down from the top of the screen. Here's how you can use it:

Basic Controls:

The Quick Settings panel gives you access to features like Wi-Fi, Bluetooth, Do Not Disturb, Airplane mode, Auto-rotate, and more. You can toggle these settings on or off with a single tap.

Customizing Quick Settings:

To personalize your Quick Settings, tap the three dots in the top-right corner of the panel, then select Edit buttons. Here, you can drag and rearrange the buttons to prioritize the ones you use most often.

You can also add new tiles for features like Dark Mode, Battery Saver, or NFC, depending on what you need.

Accessing Additional Options:

Some icons in the Quick Settings panel have additional options that can be accessed by tapping and holding. For instance, tapping and holding Wi-Fi will open the full Wi-Fi settings, allowing you to choose a network or modify additional settings.

Managing Notifications and App Permissions

Notifications keep you informed about messages, app updates, calls, and more. With the Galaxy S25 Ultra, managing and customizing notifications is quick and easy.

Viewing and Managing Notifications:

To view your notifications, swipe down from the top of the screen. From here, you can see all incoming alerts. You can also swipe left or right to dismiss notifications or tap on them to take action.

To manage notifications more effectively, go to Settings > Notifications, where you can adjust which apps can send notifications and how they appear (e.g., on the lock screen, sound, or vibrate).

Customizing Notification Alerts:

For individual apps, you can customize the notification sound, vibration, and pop-up style. This allows you to differentiate between messages, emails, and other alerts.

You can also set Do Not Disturb mode to silence notifications at specific times, or allow only certain apps or contacts to send alerts.

App Permissions:

To manage app permissions, go to Settings > Apps. Here, you can select any app and modify its permissions, such as access to your location, camera, microphone, or contacts. This ensures that apps only have the necessary permissions, keeping your data secure.

Customizing Do Not Disturb and Screen Brightness

Do Not Disturb Mode:

This feature silences all alerts to help you stay focused or sleep better. To activate it, swipe down the Quick Settings panel and toggle the Do Not Disturb icon.

You can schedule Do Not Disturb to activate at specific times (e.g., at night) by going to Settings > Sounds and vibration > Do Not Disturb.

Adjusting Screen Brightness:

The Galaxy S25 Ultra features an adaptive brightness setting, which automatically adjusts the screen brightness based on ambient lighting. However, you can adjust the brightness manually by swiping down on the Quick Settings panel and adjusting the brightness slider.

You can also enable Blue Light Filter (night mode) from the Quick Settings panel to reduce eye strain in low-light conditions.

Personalizing Your Galaxy S25 Ultra

Your Galaxy S25 Ultra is fully customizable to match your style and preferences. From changing the look of the interface to enhancing your viewing experience, here's how you can personalize your device.

Changing Themes and Wallpapers

Themes:

To change the overall look of your Galaxy S25 Ultra, go to Settings > Themes. Here, you can download new themes from the Samsung Themes store, which include wallpapers, icons, and overall color schemes.

You can also create your own theme or use the default options like Light or Dark Mode.

Wallpapers:

To change your wallpaper, long press on the home screen and select Wallpapers. You can choose from the default Samsung wallpapers, your own photos, or a range of live wallpapers for dynamic visual effects.

Adjusting System Fonts and Icons

Changing Font Style and Size:

To change the font style and size, go to Settings > Display > Font and screen zoom. You can choose a font style from the default options or download new ones from the Samsung Store. You can also adjust the font size and screen zoom to make text easier to read.

Changing Icon Size:

To adjust icon size, go to Settings > Display > Home screen. Here, you can resize icons and adjust their layout, allowing you to fit more apps on your home screen.

Enabling Dark Mode for a Comfortable Viewing Experience

Dark Mode is one of the most popular features of modern Android devices, and the Galaxy S25 Ultra supports it fully. Dark Mode reduces eye strain, saves battery life on OLED displays, and looks sleek.

Activating Dark Mode:

To enable Dark Mode, go to Settings > Display and toggle the Dark Mode option.

Scheduling Dark Mode:

You can also schedule Dark Mode to automatically turn on at sunset and turn off at sunrise by selecting the Turn on as scheduled option.

Navigating the interface of your Samsung Galaxy S25 Ultra is the first step in making this powerful device your own. Whether it's customizing the home screen, managing notifications, or changing the overall look of the device, the S25 Ultra offers a wealth of personalization options to suit your preferences. By understanding these features, you can create an experience that enhances your productivity, entertainment, and overall enjoyment.

The flexibility and customization options available make the Galaxy S25 Ultra a highly personalized and dynamic device, perfectly suited to meet your individual needs. With this guide, you're well on your way to becoming an expert user, capable of maximizing the potential of every aspect of your Galaxy S25 Ultra. Happy exploring!

CHAPTER 3

Exploring the Camera System of the Samsung Galaxy S25 Ultra

The Samsung Galaxy S25 Ultra sets a new standard in mobile photography with its 200MP main camera and advanced quad-camera system. Whether you are a casual photographer or an experienced professional, the S25 Ultra offers a host of features designed to capture stunning photos and videos in any situation. From high-resolution stills to cinematic video quality, the Galaxy S25 Ultra's camera system has been engineered for those who demand nothing but the best. In this chapter, we will explore the full range of features offered by the Galaxy S25 Ultra's camera system, providing you with tips, techniques, and settings to take your photography to the next level.

The Power of 200MP Camera: Introduction to the S25 Ultra's Camera System

The camera system in the Samsung Galaxy S25 Ultra is undoubtedly one of the standout features of the device. With its powerful 200MP main sensor, dual telephoto lenses, and ultra-wide lens, this smartphone offers unparalleled photography capabilities. Let's break down the quad-camera system and understand what makes each component so important for delivering incredible image quality.

Overview of the Quad-Camera System

The quad-camera system on the Galaxy S25 Ultra consists of the following lenses:

200MP Main Sensor: The centerpiece of the S25 Ultra's camera setup, this incredibly high-resolution sensor captures images with extraordinary detail. This sensor is designed for professional-grade photos, offering sharpness, clarity, and the ability to crop without losing quality.

12MP Ultra-Wide Lens: For expansive landscape shots or group photos, the ultra-wide lens lets you capture a wider field of view without distortion. It's perfect for architectural photography, scenic views, and tight spaces where you need to capture everything in one shot.

10MP Telephoto Lens (3x Optical Zoom): The telephoto lens allows for optical zoom, bringing distant subjects closer without sacrificing image quality. With 3x optical zoom, you can zoom into a subject from a considerable distance while maintaining clarity and sharpness.

10MP Periscope Telephoto Lens (10x Optical Zoom): The periscope-style telephoto lens gives you an incredible 10x optical zoom, allowing you to capture distant subjects in high resolution. This lens is particularly useful for sports, wildlife, or any scenario where you need to zoom in without losing clarity.

Together, these lenses allow the Galaxy S25 Ultra to excel in a wide variety of shooting conditions, offering an incredible range of zoom, detail, and depth that surpasses most smartphones on the market.

Understanding the Telephoto and Ultra-Wide Lenses

The telephoto and ultra-wide lenses are essential for expanding your creative possibilities when using the S25 Ultra's camera. Here's how each lens can be used to its fullest potential:

Telephoto Lens (3x Optical Zoom): Perfect for subjects at a medium distance, the telephoto lens gives you the ability to capture far-off objects without the loss of detail that occurs with digital zoom. When used in conjunction with the 200MP main sensor, you can zoom in on distant subjects and still retain high image quality. This is ideal for capturing portraits or shooting wildlife in the distance.

Ultra-Wide Lens (12MP): If you're taking photos in tight spaces or want to capture sweeping landscapes, the ultra-wide lens comes in handy. It provides a 120-degree field of view, letting you capture expansive scenes in one frame. The low distortion of the lens ensures that wide-angle shots look natural and true to life, even when photographing architectural or landscape subjects.

Using the 200MP Main Sensor for Professional Photography

The 200MP main sensor is the star of the S25 Ultra's camera system, and it allows you to take incredibly detailed photos. Whether you're shooting landscapes, close-ups, or portraits, this sensor captures every detail in stunning clarity. Here's how to make the most of this powerful camera:

High-Resolution Photography: The 200MP sensor captures vast amounts of detail in each photo. If you're taking photos in high-light settings, such as the outdoors during the day, you'll notice that the image retains detail even when you zoom in or crop the image. This is particularly useful when you need to print large-scale photos or crop the image while maintaining clarity.

Image Sharpness and Clarity: The 200MP sensor produces images with incredible sharpness and clarity. The sensor uses non-binned pixels, meaning it captures more light and detail per pixel, producing vibrant and well-defined shots.

Pro Mode: When you use Pro Mode, you unlock manual controls like ISO, shutter speed, and white balance, allowing you to adjust the exposure and focus for professional-level results. By customizing these settings, you can take full control of how the camera captures light, shadows, and depth.

Capturing Stunning Photos and Videos

The Samsung Galaxy S25 Ultra camera system allows you to capture stunning photos and videos in virtually any lighting condition. Whether you're shooting in broad daylight, at sunset, or in low-light environments, the S25 Ultra provides options to ensure your photos and videos look their best.

Pro Tips for Taking Amazing Photos in Different Lighting Conditions

Lighting plays a crucial role in photography, and the Galaxy S25 Ultra has features that help optimize shots in various lighting conditions:

Bright Daylight: In bright daylight, use the Ultra-Wide Lens to capture sweeping landscapes, or the 200MP main sensor to capture fine details. Avoid overexposing your photos by adjusting the ISO and exposure manually in Pro Mode.

Low Light: The Night Mode is perfect for capturing clear, bright photos in low-light conditions. The Galaxy S25 Ultra's f/1.8 aperture and high ISO capabilities help capture more light, resulting in clear and detailed photos, even in near-darkness.

Portraits: Use the Telephoto Lens for stunning portraits with a blurred background (bokeh effect). You can adjust the depth of field to ensure your subject stands out sharply against the soft background.

How to Shoot in 8K Video and the Advantages of High-Resolution Filming

One of the standout features of the S25 Ultra is its ability to shoot 8K video at 24fps. This high-resolution filming is ideal for professional-grade video recording, offering crisp detail and clarity that can be cropped and edited without losing quality.

8K Video Resolution: With 7680 x 4320 pixels, the 8K video on the S25 Ultra delivers a level of detail that is unmatched in mobile filmmaking. Whether you're recording nature, sports, or dynamic scenes, the ultra-high resolution ensures that every moment is captured in vivid detail.

Advantages of 8K Video:

Future-Proof: As more platforms and devices adopt 8K support, shooting in 8K ensures that your videos are future-ready.

Post-Production Flexibility: With such high resolution, you can crop and reframe your shots in post-production without losing detail. This makes it easier to adjust compositions or create slow-motion effects from high-quality footage.

Pro Tips for 8K Video:

Keep your camera steady or use Super Steady Video mode for smooth footage, as 8K filming can highlight any minor shakes.

Focus on lighting, as 8K videos tend to show noise in low-light environments. Use additional lighting for better clarity.

Using Night Mode for Low-Light Environments

Capturing photos in low-light environments has always been a challenge for smartphones, but the Galaxy S25 Ultra has made great strides in this area. With Night Mode, you can take clear, detailed photos even in near-darkness.

How Night Mode Works: The Night Mode feature uses longer exposure times to gather more light, while AI automatically reduces noise and enhances image clarity. The result is a sharper, brighter image, even in environments with minimal lighting.

Pro Tips for Night Photography:

Stabilize Your Camera: Keep your phone still while the camera captures the image over a longer exposure. A tripod or steady surface can help improve image quality.

Adjust Exposure: In Night Mode, try adjusting the exposure for better brightness. The S25 Ultra's AI helps maintain detail in highlights and shadows.

Camera Modes and Settings

The Galaxy S25 Ultra offers several advanced camera modes and settings that help you capture the best possible photo or video, no matter the subject or environment.

Learning About Single Take, Pro Mode, and Super Steady Video

Single Take Mode:

This is an exciting feature that lets you take multiple photos and videos at once with just a single press of the shutter button. The camera uses AI to analyze the scene and capture different formats, including wide-angle shots, close-ups, and video clips. It's perfect for those times when you want to capture a variety of moments in one go.

Pro Mode:

For users who want complete control over their shots, Pro Mode allows you to adjust manual settings such as ISO, shutter speed, white balance, and exposure. With Pro Mode, you can experiment with light, composition, and focus for professional-level results. This is ideal for photographers who want to fine-tune every aspect of their image.

Super Steady Video:

Super Steady video mode stabilizes shaky footage, making it ideal for action shots or recording while moving. The S25 Ultra uses AI-powered stabilization to ensure your video remains smooth and clear, even during intense motion.

AI-Driven Scene Optimization and How It Works

The Galaxy S25 Ultra uses AI-powered scene optimization to automatically adjust camera settings based on the subject you're photographing. Whether you're capturing food, landscapes, portraits, or animals, the AI analyzes the scene and applies the best settings for optimal results.

Scene Detection: The camera can identify over 30 different scenes and adjust settings such as contrast, saturation, and brightness for the best possible shot.

Real-Time Adjustments: AI makes real-time adjustments to focus, lighting, and exposure, so you don't have to worry about fine-tuning settings during your shoot.

Adjusting Settings Like ISO, White Balance, and Exposure in Pro Mode

For those who want more control, Pro Mode allows you to manually adjust a variety of settings:

ISO: The ISO setting determines the camera's sensitivity to light. Higher ISO values are useful in low-light situations but can introduce noise. For optimal quality, use the lowest ISO possible for well-lit environments and increase it only when necessary.

White Balance: White balance affects the color temperature of your photos. Adjusting white balance helps remove color casts from images, ensuring that colors look natural. The S25 Ultra offers several presets for different lighting conditions, such as Daylight, Cloudy, and Incandescent.

Shutter Speed: Shutter speed controls how long the camera's sensor is exposed to light. A faster shutter speed freezes motion, while a slower shutter speed creates motion blur. Slower speeds are useful for long exposure shots, such as waterfalls or night photography.

The Samsung Galaxy S25 Ultra's camera system is a game-changer for mobile photography, offering a suite of powerful features that rival professional cameras. Whether you're using the 200MP main sensor to capture incredible detail, the telephoto lenses for zooming into distant subjects, or the ultra-wide lens for expansive shots, the S25 Ultra makes it easier than ever to capture stunning images and videos. With advanced features like Pro Mode, AI-driven scene optimization, and Super Steady Video, this device offers a versatile, all-in-one solution for your creative needs.

Armed with this knowledge, you are ready to dive into the world of mobile photography and capture moments like never before. The Samsung Galaxy S25 Ultra gives you the tools to turn ordinary photos into extraordinary works of art, making it an essential device for photographers and content creators alike. Happy shooting!

CHAPTER 4

Managing Battery Life and Charging on the Samsung Galaxy S25 Ultra

The Samsung Galaxy S25 Ultra is a powerhouse of technology, offering incredible performance, a stunning display, and professional-grade cameras. However, all these features require power. Managing battery life effectively is key to ensuring that your phone can keep up with your demands throughout the day. In this chapter, we'll explore various ways to charge your device efficiently, maximize battery life, and make the most of the power-saving features on the Galaxy S25 Ultra.

Charging Your Galaxy S25 Ultra

Understanding how to charge your Galaxy S25 Ultra correctly will ensure that your device performs optimally while maintaining long-term battery health. The S25 Ultra supports both fast charging and wireless charging, offering you flexibility depending on your needs.

Fast Charging (45W) vs. Wireless Charging (15W)

One of the most impressive features of the Galaxy S25 Ultra is its 45W fast charging capability. This technology allows the device to recharge quickly, so you can spend less time plugged in and more time using your device. Let's break down the two primary charging methods supported by the S25 Ultra:

Fast Charging (45W)

45W fast charging is one of the fastest charging methods available on smartphones today. With this capability, the Galaxy S25 Ultra can charge up to 50% in just 30 minutes. This is ideal for users who need to charge their phone quickly during a short break, whether at work, in the car, or at the airport.

How it Works: Fast charging uses higher wattage to supply more power to the device, which reduces the time it takes to charge the battery. The S25 Ultra supports USB-C fast charging, so you'll need to use a USB-C to USB-C cable that is compatible with 45W charging.

Best for: This charging method is perfect when you need your device charged quickly. For example, if you forgot to charge your phone overnight and need a quick boost, 45W fast charging will have your phone up and running in no time.

Wireless Charging (15W)

Wireless charging allows you to charge your phone without physically plugging in a cable. The Galaxy S25 Ultra supports 15W wireless charging, offering a less speedy, but still efficient, method of recharging your device. To use wireless charging, you'll need a Qi-compatible wireless charger that supports 15W charging.

How it Works: Wireless charging works by transferring energy from the charging pad to your phone's battery via electromagnetic induction. While slower than fast charging, it's convenient for use at home, at work, or anywhere you can place your phone on a charging pad.

Best for: Wireless charging is best used when you want to avoid dealing with cables or when your phone is stationary on a desk or nightstand. It's also ideal for overnight charging or when you're not in a rush.

Important Tip: While wireless charging is convenient, it generates more heat than wired charging, which could slightly affect battery longevity over time. For optimal battery health, it's recommended to use wireless charging intermittently and rely on wired charging when you need a quick top-up.

How to Use Wireless PowerShare to Charge Other Devices

One of the unique features of the Galaxy S25 Ultra is Wireless PowerShare, which allows you to wirelessly charge other devices, such as Samsung Galaxy Buds, smartwatches, or even other smartphones, using your phone's battery.

How it Works:

Activate Wireless PowerShare:

To enable Wireless PowerShare, swipe down from the top of the screen to access the Quick Settings panel. Look for the Wireless PowerShare icon and tap it to turn it on.

Position the Devices:

To charge another device, place it on the back of the Galaxy S25 Ultra. Align the device's charging coil with your phone's charging area (typically near the center of the back of the phone).

Charging: Once the other device is properly aligned, your S25 Ultra will begin transferring power to the device. You'll see a notification confirming that Wireless PowerShare is active, and the other device will start charging.

Best for:

Wireless PowerShare is great when you need to charge a low-battery device, like Galaxy Buds or a smartwatch, and you don't have a charging pad or separate cable available. It's also useful for charging a friend's phone in a pinch.

Choosing the Right Charger for Your Device

To get the best performance from your Galaxy S25 Ultra, it's essential to use the right charging accessories. Here's a quick guide on choosing the right charger:

Fast Charger: To use the 45W fast charging feature, make sure you use a 45W USB-C charger (Samsung's official 45W Super Fast Charger is recommended). Using a charger that supports Quick Charge 3.0 or higher ensures faster charging speeds.

Wireless Charger: If you prefer wireless charging, ensure that the charger is Qi-compatible and supports 15W or higher for faster charging speeds. For optimal results, look for the Samsung Wireless Charger Duo for faster wireless charging speeds.

Avoid Cheap Chargers: While third-party chargers may seem like a cost-effective solution, they can often lead to slower charging speeds, overheating, or even damage to your device. Always choose chargers from reputable brands or those certified by Samsung.

Maximizing Battery Life

While the Samsung Galaxy S25 Ultra is equipped with an impressive battery capacity, it's important to manage your battery to ensure it lasts throughout the day. Here are some tips and techniques to maximize your battery life:

Tips to Extend Battery Life Throughout the Day

Reduce Screen Brightness: One of the most power-hungry components of any phone is the display. Reducing the screen brightness or enabling Adaptive Brightness helps conserve power. Adaptive Brightness automatically adjusts your screen's brightness based on the ambient light and your usage patterns.

Turn Off Unused Features: If you're not using features like Bluetooth, GPS, or Wi-Fi, it's a good idea to turn them off. This helps conserve battery by reducing background processes.

Limit Background Apps: Many apps run in the background, consuming both battery and data. Regularly close unused apps or go to Settings > Battery and device care > Battery to check which apps are using the most power.

Use Power Saving Mode: The Galaxy S25 Ultra offers different levels of Power Saving Mode that reduce background activities, lower screen brightness, and limit performance to extend battery life.

Avoid Overcharging: Though modern smartphones like the S25 Ultra are designed to prevent overcharging, it's still a good practice to unplug your phone once it reaches 100%. Charging to around 80% and avoiding keeping it plugged in all the time can help preserve the long-term health of your battery.

Optimize App Usage: Apps like social media and streaming services can use significant amounts of battery. Limiting app notifications, disabling background updates, or using Lite versions of apps can help reduce power consumption.

Optimizing Settings for Long-Lasting Performance

The S25 Ultra offers several built-in settings to optimize battery life:

Adaptive Battery: This feature uses AI to monitor your battery usage and adapts by limiting power to apps you don't use often. Enable Adaptive Battery in Settings > Battery and device care > Battery > Adaptive Battery.

Battery Saver Mode: If you're running low on battery and don't have immediate access to a charger, turning on Battery Saver Mode can extend the battery life by reducing screen brightness, limiting background data, and disabling non-essential features. You can activate it manually or schedule it to kick in when the battery drops to a certain level.

Dark Mode: As previously mentioned, enabling Dark Mode on your Galaxy S25 Ultra reduces the energy consumption of the AMOLED screen, as dark pixels use less power than bright ones. You can activate Dark Mode through Settings > Display > Dark Mode.

App Power Management: App power management helps limit apps that use a lot of power in the background. Go to Settings > Battery and device care > Battery > Power saving mode to see which apps are draining your battery and restrict their activities.

Understanding Battery Usage Statistics

The Galaxy S25 Ultra provides detailed statistics on how your battery is being used. Here's how to check your battery usage:

Go to Settings > Battery and device care > Battery.

Under Battery usage, you'll see a breakdown of which apps or services are using the most battery.

You can view screen on time versus screen off time, allowing you to identify power-hungry apps or settings.

By reviewing these statistics regularly, you can identify apps or habits that may be draining your battery faster than necessary and take steps to improve your battery performance.

Power Saving Features

In addition to fast charging, the Samsung Galaxy S25 Ultra comes equipped with various power-saving features to help conserve battery life throughout the day. Let's take a closer look at these options:

Enabling Adaptive Battery for Smarter Usage

As mentioned earlier, Adaptive Battery is a built-in feature that helps extend your battery life. Here's how it works:

How It Works: Adaptive Battery uses AI to learn your usage patterns. It identifies which apps you use most frequently and ensures that they get priority access to the battery, while apps you rarely use are restricted from consuming power in the background.

Enabling Adaptive Battery: To enable Adaptive Battery, go to Settings > Battery and device care > Battery and toggle the Adaptive Battery option.

Using Power Saving Mode to Reduce Battery Consumption

Power Saving Mode is a great way to ensure that your Galaxy S25 Ultra lasts longer when you need it the most. You can choose from different levels of power-saving modes to suit your needs:

Medium Power Saving: This reduces background activity, lowers screen brightness, and limits app performance to save battery.

Maximum Power Saving: This dramatically reduces performance, turns off non-essential features (like animations and background syncing), and restricts apps to only essential functions.

To enable Power Saving Mode, go to Settings > Battery and device care > Battery > Power saving mode.

Managing Background Apps and System Resources

Many apps continue to run in the background, consuming power and resources. Managing these apps efficiently can help extend battery life. Here's how:

Background App Management: Go to Settings > Battery and device care > Battery > Background usage limits. From here, you can set limits for specific apps, ensuring they don't consume battery unnecessarily.

App Standby: The Galaxy S25 Ultra uses App Standby to limit the power usage of apps that are not in active use. If an app hasn't been used in a while, it will automatically be put into standby mode, reducing its battery usage.

The Samsung Galaxy S25 Ultra offers a variety of charging methods and power-saving features to help you manage battery life and keep your device performing optimally. By understanding how fast charging, wireless charging, and power-saving modes work, you can ensure that your phone remains ready to tackle whatever you throw at it.

Whether you're powering through the day with fast charging, managing battery usage with Adaptive Battery, or using Power Saving Mode to eke out the last bit of charge, the S25 Ultra's powerful features are designed to keep you connected and productive for as long as possible. By following the tips and tricks provided in this guide, you'll be able to maximize your Galaxy S25 Ultra's battery life and keep it running smoothly throughout the day.

CHAPTER 5

Advanced Features and Customization of the Samsung Galaxy S25 Ultra

The Samsung Galaxy S25 Ultra offers a range of advanced features and customization options that allow you to truly make the device your own. With S Pen functionality, multi-window multitasking, and the ability to transform your phone into a desktop PC with Samsung DeX, the Galaxy S25 Ultra provides a powerful and flexible platform for work, creativity, and entertainment. In this chapter, we will explore these features in depth, giving you the tools to maximize the potential of your device and streamline your daily activities.

S Pen Features (Exclusive to S25 Ultra)

One of the standout features of the Samsung Galaxy S25 Ultra is the S Pen—a powerful tool designed to enhance productivity, creativity, and precision. With its advanced capabilities, the S Pen brings a new level of functionality to the Galaxy S25 Ultra, making it perfect for everything from note-taking to editing documents, creating art, and controlling your device remotely. Let's dive into the S Pen's features and how to use them effectively.

Setting Up and Using the S Pen for Quick Notes and Sketches

The S Pen is conveniently stored within the Galaxy S25 Ultra, sliding into a dedicated slot at the bottom of the phone. To begin using it, simply remove the S Pen from its slot, and the phone will automatically detect the pen, readying the device for use.

Creating Quick Notes:

One of the most practical uses of the S Pen is for quick note-taking. With the Screen Off Memo feature, you can write notes without even unlocking your phone.

To use Screen Off Memo, simply remove the S Pen and start writing on the screen while it's turned off. Your notes will be saved instantly in the Notes app, allowing you to access them later.

Sketching and Drawing:

The S Pen is not just for writing—it's also a powerful tool for sketching and drawing. Whether you're creating digital art, doodling for fun, or taking down detailed diagrams, the S Pen offers a precise and responsive writing experience.

Use the Samsung Notes app to create a new drawing. You can choose from a variety of pens and brushes and adjust their size and opacity to create the perfect sketch. The pressure sensitivity of the S Pen allows for nuanced strokes, giving you the feeling of writing or drawing with a real pen or pencil.

Saving and Organizing Notes:

All the notes and sketches you create with the S Pen are stored in Samsung Notes. From there, you can organize them by creating different notebooks, categorize them by topic, and even convert handwritten text to digital text for easier search and editing.

Air Actions: Using the S Pen Remotely for Gestures

The Air Actions feature of the S Pen adds an extra layer of functionality, allowing you to perform gestures without physically touching the screen. Using Bluetooth connectivity, the S Pen becomes a remote control for your Galaxy S25 Ultra. This is perfect for presentations, media playback, or taking photos without having to touch your device.

Using Air Actions for Media Control:

For media playback, you can use Air Actions to pause or play music, skip tracks, or adjust the volume without needing to touch the screen. Simply point the S Pen at the screen and use the assigned gestures (e.g., swiping left or right or pressing the button on the pen).

Camera Control:

When taking photos or videos, you can use Air Actions to remotely capture images or start/stop video recording. Point the S Pen towards the camera and click the button to take a photo, or perform other gestures to zoom in and out or switch between camera modes.

Customizing Air Actions:

You can customize the gestures for different apps and functions in the S Pen settings. Go to Settings > Advanced features > S Pen > Air actions to assign specific functions to each gesture. This allows for a personalized experience, making your device even more efficient.

How to Create and Interact with the Notes App Using the S Pen

The Samsung Notes app is the central hub for all your notes, sketches, and creative work. The S Pen enhances this app by offering an intuitive and precise way to interact with your content. Let's explore how you can make the most of the Notes app with your S Pen.

Creating and Editing Notes:

Open the Samsung Notes app and choose from a variety of note types, including text, voice recordings, images, and handwritten notes. When you write, the S Pen offers incredible precision, allowing for comfortable, natural writing.

Syncing Notes Across Devices:

If you use other Samsung devices, your notes will automatically sync through your Samsung account. This makes it easy to access and edit your notes across multiple devices, ensuring that your information is always up to date.

Organizing and Sharing Notes:

You can organize your notes into notebooks, making it easy to categorize and retrieve your content later. You can also share notes with others via email or messaging apps or export them as PDFs or images for easier sharing and collaboration.

Multi-Window and Split-Screen Mode

The Galaxy S25 Ultra allows you to multitask seamlessly with Multi-Window Mode and Split-Screen Mode. These features allow you to run two apps at the same time, improving your efficiency and productivity. Let's explore how to use these features effectively.

How to Run Two Apps Simultaneously with Multi-Window Mode

Multi-Window Mode enables you to open and use two apps side by side, allowing for more efficient multitasking. Whether you're responding to emails while browsing the web or taking notes during a video call, Multi-Window Mode makes it easy to split your screen into two distinct sections.

Activating Multi-Window Mode:

To use Multi-Window Mode, open an app and then swipe up from the bottom of the screen to access the recent apps menu.

Tap the app icon at the top of the screen and select Open in split screen view.

Choose a second app from the recent apps list to open it in the other half of the screen.

Adjusting the Window Size:

You can adjust the size of the windows by dragging the divider between the two apps. This allows you to give more space to one app while keeping the other accessible.

Closing Apps in Multi-Window Mode:

To close an app in Multi-Window Mode, simply drag the dividing line all the way to the edge of the screen, and the app will close. You can also press the back button to exit Multi-Window Mode.

Setting Up App Pairing for Your Favorite Dual-App Combinations

If you frequently use certain apps together, you can set up App Pairing for easy access. This feature allows you to create a shortcut that opens two apps in Split-Screen Mode with a single tap.

Creating an App Pair:

Go to Settings > Display > Edge panels and enable the Apps edge.

Tap the Edge panel handle on the side of the screen, and select the App Pair icon.

Choose the two apps you want to pair, and they will appear as a shortcut in the Edge panel.

Using App Pair:

To use the App Pair, simply tap the shortcut in the Edge panel, and the two apps will open simultaneously in Split-Screen Mode. This feature is ideal for users who regularly multitask, allowing for a seamless and efficient workflow.

Managing Split-Screen Settings for Productivity

Split-Screen Mode helps boost your productivity by allowing you to use two apps at the same time. To further optimize your experience, you can tweak Split-Screen settings:

Adjust the Aspect Ratio: Some apps allow you to adjust their aspect ratio for a better view in Split-Screen Mode. If the app's interface doesn't fit well in a narrow window, you can modify the app's view to make it more usable.

Disable Split-Screen Mode: If you don't want to use two apps simultaneously, you can quickly disable Split-Screen Mode by pressing the recent apps button and selecting Close all.

Samsung DeX: Turn Your Galaxy S25 Ultra into a Desktop

Samsung DeX is a revolutionary feature that turns your Galaxy S25 Ultra into a full-fledged desktop PC. With DeX, you can use your phone's apps on a larger screen, making it easier to multitask, work, and enjoy entertainment in a desktop-like experience. Let's explore how to set up and use Samsung DeX for productivity, gaming, and entertainment.

Setting Up and Using Samsung DeX for a PC-Like Experience

Samsung DeX is perfect for users who need a PC-like environment while on the go. Here's how to set it up:

Connecting to a Monitor:

You can connect your Galaxy S25 Ultra to a monitor using a USB-C to HDMI cable or a DeX-compatible dock. Simply plug one end into your phone and the other into the HDMI port of a monitor, TV, or projector.

You can also use a wireless connection by using Wi-Fi to connect your phone to a smart TV or wireless DeX station.

Using a Keyboard and Mouse:

To enhance the DeX experience, connect a Bluetooth keyboard and mouse to your Galaxy S25 Ultra. Once paired, you can control the device just like a traditional desktop.

Alternatively, you can use a USB-C hub to connect wired peripherals.

DeX Interface:

Once connected, the DeX interface will appear on the monitor. You can open apps in windows, resize them, and interact with them using your mouse and keyboard, just like a computer.

The DeX interface is optimized for productivity, allowing you to run multiple apps simultaneously, switch between them, and drag-and-drop content between apps.

Optimizing DeX for Work, Gaming, and Entertainment

DeX is a powerful tool for various tasks. Whether you need to use your phone for work, gaming, or entertainment, DeX has you covered:

Productivity:

You can use Microsoft Office apps (Word, Excel, PowerPoint), Google Docs, and Samsung Notes for office work. You can also access emails, schedule meetings, and view documents as if you were on a desktop computer.

Samsung DeX supports drag-and-drop functionality, making it easier to move files between apps or open multiple documents simultaneously.

Gaming:

DeX can turn your Galaxy S25 Ultra into a gaming station. Connect to a larger screen and use your Bluetooth gamepad for console-like gaming. Enjoy your favorite mobile games on a bigger screen with smoother graphics and controls.

Entertainment:

DeX is also great for streaming media. You can watch videos from apps like YouTube, Netflix, and Disney+ on a larger screen, while using your phone for other tasks in the background. Additionally, you can mirror content from your phone directly to your TV using Samsung DeX for a seamless entertainment experience.

The Samsung Galaxy S25 Ultra is packed with advanced features and customization options that enhance your productivity, creativity, and entertainment. From the precision of the S Pen to the multitasking power of Multi-Window Mode, and the ability to turn your phone into a desktop PC with Samsung DeX, the Galaxy S25 Ultra offers everything you need to get the most out of your device.

Whether you're a creative professional looking to draw and take notes, a gamer wanting to use your phone as a gaming hub, or a business user needing a desktop experience on the go, the S25 Ultra adapts to your needs. With its wealth of features and customization options, this phone is more than just a device—it's a tool designed to enhance and streamline every aspect of your digital life.

By mastering these advanced features, you'll be able to make your Galaxy S25 Ultra truly your own, boosting your efficiency, creativity, and enjoyment in ways you never thought possible.

CHAPTER 6

Connectivity and Network Settings on the Samsung Galaxy S25 Ultra

In today's world, staying connected is more important than ever. The Samsung Galaxy S25 Ultra provides a suite of connectivity options that ensure you're always connected, whether you're at home, on the go, or at work. From Wi-Fi to Bluetooth, 5G, and mobile hotspots, the Galaxy S25 Ultra ensures you have the speed and flexibility to handle all your connectivity needs. Additionally, the device includes features such as NFC and Samsung Pay, which enable secure, contactless payments for easy transactions.

In this chapter, we will guide you through setting up and managing all these features, as well as troubleshooting common issues you might encounter along the way. Let's dive into how to get the most out of your connectivity and network settings on the Galaxy S25 Ultra.

Setting Up Wi-Fi, Bluetooth, and Mobile Networks

The Galaxy S25 Ultra supports multiple ways to connect to the internet, devices, and mobile networks. Whether you're connecting to a home Wi-Fi network, managing Bluetooth devices, or using 5G for ultra-fast mobile data, this phone is designed to make connectivity easy and fast.

How to Connect to Wi-Fi and Troubleshoot Connectivity Issues

Wi-Fi is one of the most common ways to stay connected, and the Galaxy S25 Ultra makes it easy to join networks and troubleshoot common connectivity issues. Here's how to set up Wi-Fi and handle any issues that may arise:

Connecting to Wi-Fi:

Step 1: Open the Settings app on your Galaxy S25 Ultra.

Step 2: Scroll down and tap on Connections.

Step 3: Select Wi-Fi, and ensure that Wi-Fi is turned on.

Step 4: Your device will automatically scan for available networks. Tap the network you wish to join and enter the password if required. If the network is secured with a password, you'll need to enter it.

Step 5: Once connected, your Wi-Fi icon will appear in the status bar at the top of the screen.

Troubleshooting Wi-Fi Issues:

If you're having trouble connecting to a Wi-Fi network, try the following:

Restart your device: Sometimes, restarting the phone can resolve minor connectivity issues.

Restart your router: If other devices are also having trouble connecting, the issue might be with your router.

Forget and reconnect: If the Wi-Fi network is not connecting, go to Settings > Connections > Wi-Fi, tap the gear icon next to the network, and select Forget. Afterward, reconnect by entering the password again.

Check your router settings: Ensure that your router is configured properly and that it supports the right frequency bands (2.4 GHz or 5 GHz).

Advanced Wi-Fi Settings:

To optimize your Wi-Fi experience, you can configure advanced settings. Go to Settings > Connections > Wi-Fi > Advanced and explore features such as Wi-Fi Direct, Wi-Fi Calling, and Switch to mobile data when the Wi-Fi signal is weak.

Managing Bluetooth Devices like Headphones, Speakers, and Wearables

The Galaxy S25 Ultra is equipped with the latest Bluetooth technology, allowing you to connect to various devices, including headphones, speakers, and wearables. Whether you're listening to music, answering calls, or syncing your fitness tracker, Bluetooth connectivity is key for a wireless experience.

Connecting Bluetooth Devices:

Step 1: Open Settings on your device and select Connections.

Step 2: Tap Bluetooth, and ensure that Bluetooth is turned on.

Step 3: Your device will begin scanning for nearby Bluetooth devices. Select the device you want to connect to (e.g., headphones, smartwatch, or Bluetooth speaker).

Step 4: Follow any prompts to complete the connection, which may include entering a passcode or pairing number.

Managing Connected Devices:

Once your devices are connected, you can manage them in the Bluetooth settings. Tap the device name to adjust settings such as audio output, volume, and notifications. You can also set the device to connect automatically when it's in range.

Troubleshooting Bluetooth Issues:

Check device compatibility: Ensure that the Bluetooth device you are trying to connect to is compatible with your phone.

Reconnect devices: If you're having trouble connecting, try turning Bluetooth off and on again on your Galaxy S25 Ultra, or turn your Bluetooth device off and on.

Forget and reconnect: Go to Settings > Connections > Bluetooth, select the device, and tap Forget. Then try reconnecting it from scratch.

Enabling and Managing 5G for Ultra-Fast Mobile Data

The Samsung Galaxy S25 Ultra supports 5G, the next generation of mobile internet technology. With 5G, you can enjoy faster download speeds, smoother streaming, and improved connectivity. Here's how to enable and manage your 5G connection:

Enabling 5G:

Step 1: Open Settings on your Galaxy S25 Ultra.

Step 2: Scroll down and select Connections.

Step 3: Tap Mobile networks > Network mode.

Step 4: Select 5G/LTE/3G/2G (auto connect). This ensures that your device will automatically switch to 5G when it's available.

Checking 5G Availability:

Not all areas have 5G coverage yet, so make sure to check if you're in an area with 5G signal. You can check the status in the status bar at the top of your screen; the 5G icon will appear when you're connected to a 5G network.

Managing 5G:

If you don't need 5G and want to conserve battery life, you can switch to 4G by selecting the appropriate option under Network mode in the mobile network settings.

Troubleshooting 5G Issues:

Weak Signal: If you experience poor 5G performance, it could be due to weak signal strength or network congestion. Try moving to a different location with better 5G coverage.

Carrier Restrictions: Ensure that your carrier supports 5G and that you have an active 5G-compatible plan.

Using the Hotspot Feature

A personal hotspot allows you to share your mobile data connection with other devices, such as laptops, tablets, or other smartphones. The Galaxy S25 Ultra makes it easy to set up and manage your own hotspot.

How to Set Up a Personal Hotspot for Sharing Data

Step 1: Open the Settings app on your Galaxy S25 Ultra.

Step 2: Tap Connections and then select Mobile hotspot and tethering.

Step 3: Tap Mobile Hotspot and toggle it to On.

Step 4: Configure your hotspot by tapping Configure. Here, you can set:

Network Name (SSID): Name your hotspot for easy identification.

Security: Set a password to secure your hotspot connection.

Network Band: Choose between 2.4 GHz and 5 GHz depending on the type of devices you plan to connect.

Step 5: Once the hotspot is configured, other devices can search for your hotspot name (SSID) and connect using the password you set.

Managing Hotspot Settings to Control Data Usage and Security

Managing the hotspot's settings is essential to ensure efficient use of your data plan and maintain security.

Data Usage Monitoring:

Go to Settings > Connections > Mobile hotspot and tethering, then tap Data usage to track how much data has been shared via the hotspot. You can set data limits to avoid overusing your mobile plan.

Security Settings:

For privacy, always enable password protection on your hotspot. Use WPA2 security for maximum encryption and security, ensuring that unauthorized devices cannot connect.

Turning Off Hotspot:

To conserve battery life or prevent others from connecting, you can turn off the hotspot by toggling it off in the Mobile hotspot and tethering section of the Settings app.

NFC and Samsung Pay

The Galaxy S25 Ultra includes NFC (Near Field Communication) for contactless payments and easy pairing with other devices. Samsung Pay leverages NFC technology, allowing you to make secure payments with just a tap of your phone. Let's explore how to set up and use NFC and Samsung Pay for a secure, fast, and convenient payment experience.

Setting Up NFC for Contactless Payments

To make use of NFC on your Galaxy S25 Ultra, you need to enable it first. Here's how:

Step 1: Open Settings and go to Connections.

Step 2: Scroll down and tap on NFC and payment.

Step 3: Toggle NFC to On.

Step 4: You can also enable Android Beam for sharing files via NFC, though it's not necessary for contactless payments.

Once NFC is enabled, you can use it to make contactless payments and share data with compatible devices.

Using Samsung Pay for a Secure and Easy Payment Experience

Samsung Pay is Samsung's secure and easy-to-use mobile payment service that allows you to pay using your phone at supported retailers. Here's how to set it up:

Step 1: Open the Samsung Pay app from your home screen or app drawer.

Step 2: Follow the on-screen prompts to add your credit card or debit card to Samsung Pay. You'll need to verify your identity by entering card details or using your fingerprint or face recognition.

Step 3: Once your card is added, you can choose to set Samsung Pay as your default payment option.

Step 4: When ready to make a purchase, simply open Samsung Pay, hold your phone near the NFC terminal, and authenticate the transaction using your fingerprint or PIN.

Troubleshooting Issues with NFC and Payment Setup

If you're having trouble using NFC or Samsung Pay, here are a few things to check:

Check NFC Settings: Ensure that NFC is enabled in Settings > Connections > NFC and payment.

Device Compatibility: Ensure that the store or vendor you're trying to pay at supports NFC payments.

Clear Samsung Pay Cache: If Samsung Pay is not working properly, go to Settings > Apps > Samsung Pay > Storage and tap Clear cache.

Card Verification: Ensure that your card has been properly verified in Samsung Pay. If not, try removing the card and adding it again.

The Samsung Galaxy S25 Ultra offers a wide array of connectivity features that allow you to stay connected, work efficiently, and manage data seamlessly. From Wi-Fi, Bluetooth, and 5G, to mobile hotspots, NFC, and Samsung Pay, these advanced features ensure that you have everything you need to stay productive and secure.

By understanding and utilizing the connectivity settings outlined in this chapter, you can optimize your phone for fast and reliable connections, and use it to its fullest potential— whether for personal, work, or entertainment purposes. Happy connecting!

CHAPTER 7

Software, Security, and Maintenance on the Samsung Galaxy S25 Ultra

The Samsung Galaxy S25 Ultra is a powerful device designed to deliver an exceptional experience, whether for work, entertainment, or creative pursuits. However, to ensure your device stays optimized, secure, and protected over time, it's essential to follow good software and maintenance practices. This chapter will guide you through keeping your Galaxy S25 Ultra secure, managing software updates, and ensuring your data is safe and recoverable when needed.

Keeping Your Device Secure

As smartphones become more integrated into our lives, security and privacy are more critical than ever. Fortunately, the Samsung Galaxy S25 Ultra offers a variety of advanced security features to protect your data, apps, and personal information. Let's explore how to set up and use these security features, including Secure Folder, the Privacy Dashboard, Samsung Knox, and more.

Setting Up Advanced Security Features Like Secure Folder and Privacy Dashboard

Secure Folder: A Secure Space for Your Personal Data

The Secure Folder feature allows you to create a private, encrypted space on your device where you can store apps, photos, files, and other sensitive information. Anything placed in the Secure Folder is protected by a separate PIN, pattern, or biometric authentication, making it much harder for unauthorized users to access your personal data.

Setting Up Secure Folder:

Go to Settings > Biometrics and security > Secure Folder.

You'll be prompted to log in to your Samsung account. If you don't have one, you'll need to create it.

Set up your authentication method, such as a PIN, pattern, or fingerprint, to protect the Secure Folder.

Using Secure Folder:

Once the folder is set up, you can add apps, photos, and documents that you want to keep private. Simply open the Secure Folder, tap Add apps or Add files, and select what you want to store.

You can also move existing apps and files into the Secure Folder, keeping everything safe and secure.

Accessing Secure Folder:

Access to the Secure Folder can be restricted by using biometric authentication (fingerprint or face recognition), ensuring that only authorized individuals can access it.

Privacy Dashboard: Monitoring App Permissions and Privacy Settings

The Privacy Dashboard is an essential tool that allows you to monitor and control the access apps have to sensitive data like your location, camera, microphone, and more. It gives you an overview of the permissions granted to each app and helps you ensure that your privacy is protected.

Accessing the Privacy Dashboard:

Go to Settings > Privacy > Privacy Dashboard.

Here, you can see a detailed view of which apps have accessed sensitive data and when.

Managing Permissions:

From the Privacy Dashboard, you can quickly revoke permissions for apps that have access to your camera, microphone, location, and other private data.

Tap on any app in the Privacy Dashboard to see what data it's accessed and adjust permissions as necessary.

This tool helps you maintain transparency and control over the apps that access your sensitive data.

Managing App Permissions and Data Sharing

In addition to the Privacy Dashboard, the Galaxy S25 Ultra offers granular control over individual app permissions. You can restrict which apps access specific features like the camera, contacts, location, and storage, ensuring that you maintain control over your data.

Managing App Permissions:

Go to Settings > Apps and select the app you want to manage.

Tap Permissions, and you'll see a list of all the features the app has access to (e.g., camera, microphone, contacts). You can toggle the permissions on or off as needed.

Data Sharing:

Samsung gives you control over how apps share data. For example, you can choose to share your location only when an app is in use, or you can prevent apps from accessing your contact list, photos, and other personal data.

Go to Settings > Privacy > Permission manager to review and control data-sharing settings for specific apps.

Using Samsung Knox for Protecting Sensitive Data

Samsung Knox is a military-grade security platform designed to protect your device from malware, hackers, and unauthorized access. It offers both hardware-based and software-based security to ensure that your personal data remains safe, even if your device is compromised.

Setting Up Samsung Knox:

Samsung Knox is integrated into the Galaxy S25 Ultra, and it runs in the background to protect your data. However, you can enhance its security by enabling Knox Vault and Secure Boot.

Go to Settings > Biometrics and security > Samsung Knox and follow the prompts to set up Knox protection.

Using Samsung Knox for Secure Data Storage:

Knox Vault allows you to store sensitive files, passwords, and personal information in a secure, encrypted environment. Access to Knox Vault is restricted by biometric authentication or a separate PIN.

Knox also works in conjunction with Secure Folder, giving you an additional layer of encryption to keep your personal information safe.

Managing Software Updates

Keeping your Samsung Galaxy S25 Ultra up to date is essential for performance improvements, new features, and security patches. Samsung provides regular updates to both the system software and apps to ensure that your device continues to run smoothly and securely.

Checking for and Installing System Updates

How to Check for System Updates:

Go to Settings > Software update > Download and install.

The device will check for the latest system updates. If there is a new update available, you can tap Download to start the update process.

Installing System Updates:

After downloading the update, the phone will prompt you to install it. Tap Install to begin the installation process.

Make sure your device has enough battery life (or is plugged into a charger) before installing an update to avoid interruptions.

Once the update is complete, your device will restart, and you'll see the new software version installed on your phone.

Setting Up Automatic Updates for Apps and System Software

To ensure that your Galaxy S25 Ultra stays up to date, you can enable automatic updates for both apps and system software:

Automatic System Updates:

Go to Settings > Software update > Auto-download over Wi-Fi. This will allow the phone to automatically download updates when connected to Wi-Fi.

Automatic App Updates:

Open the Google Play Store app and tap the hamburger menu (three horizontal lines).

Go to Settings > Auto-update apps, and choose Over Wi-Fi only or Over any network.

With this setting enabled, your apps will automatically update in the background, ensuring that your apps are always up to date with the latest features and security patches.

Clearing Cache and Optimizing Performance After Updates

After system updates or app updates, your phone might accumulate unnecessary cache files that can slow down performance. Clearing the cache and optimizing your device is a good way to maintain speed and performance.

How to Clear Cache:

Go to Settings > Apps.

Select an app, tap Storage, and tap Clear cache to remove the cached data.

Optimizing Performance:

Go to Settings > Battery and device care > Optimize now.

This tool will scan for unnecessary background apps, redundant files, and other items that might slow your phone down. Tap Optimize to clean up and improve your device's performance.

Data Backup and Recovery

Backups are critical to ensuring that your data is safe in case of device loss, damage, or system issues. The Samsung Galaxy S25 Ultra provides powerful backup options using Samsung Cloud and Google Drive, making it easy to store and restore your important data.

Using Samsung Cloud and Google Drive for Automatic Backups

Backing Up to Samsung Cloud:

Go to Settings > Accounts and backup > Samsung Cloud.

You can enable Auto Backup for your contacts, photos, messages, and other essential data. Select Backup and restore to manage and view your backups.

To initiate a backup manually, tap Back up data, choose the items to back up, and tap Back up now.

Backing Up to Google Drive:

For Google services, go to Settings > Accounts and backup > Backup and restore.

Under Google Drive, toggle Back up my data to ensure that your app data, settings, and photos are automatically backed up.

You can manage your backups by going to the Google Drive app, where you'll find the backups section, and you can see what data is being stored and restore it if necessary.

Restoring Data from Your Backup

Restoring from Samsung Cloud:

If you need to restore data, go to Settings > Accounts and backup > Samsung Cloud > Restore data.

Select the backup you wish to restore from and choose the data to recover (such as contacts, apps, or photos). Follow the on-screen prompts to complete the restoration process.

Restoring from Google Drive:

If you're restoring a device after a factory reset or need to recover app data, go to Settings > Accounts and backup > Google > Backup.

Select Restore to recover your data from Google Drive.

Factory Reset: When and How to Reset Your Device to Default Settings

A factory reset erases all data from your device, returning it to its original, out-of-the-box state. This is typically used when you want to clear your phone of personal information before selling it, or if the phone is experiencing significant software issues.

Performing a Factory Reset:

Go to Settings > General management > Reset.

Select Factory data reset, then tap Reset.

Confirm your decision by tapping Delete all. If you have a PIN or password set, you will be prompted to enter it to complete the process.

The phone will restart and begin the factory reset. This process may take several minutes.

Restoring Data After Factory Reset:

After the reset, you'll be prompted to set up the phone again. You can restore data from your backups made earlier using Samsung Cloud or Google Drive.

The Samsung Galaxy S25 Ultra is a highly secure and efficient device, and it's important to stay on top of software updates, backup strategies, and security settings to ensure optimal performance. By setting up advanced security features like Secure Folder, managing app permissions, and utilizing Samsung Knox, you can protect your data and personal information. Additionally, using cloud-based backup solutions ensures that your data remains safe, even in the event of device failure or loss.

With software updates, cache clearing, and performance optimizations, you can maintain a smooth user experience, keeping your device up to date and running at peak performance. Finally, understanding how to perform a factory reset and restore your data gives you peace of mind knowing that you can always recover your information when necessary.

By following the tips and recommendations outlined in this chapter, you'll ensure that your Samsung Galaxy S25 Ultra stays secure, optimized, and ready for whatever tasks lie ahead.

CHAPTER 8

Troubleshooting Common Issues on the Samsung Galaxy S25 Ultra

The Samsung Galaxy S25 Ultra is a sophisticated and powerful device designed to offer users an exceptional mobile experience. However, like any high-tech gadget, it is not immune to occasional issues. Fortunately, the Galaxy S25 Ultra comes equipped with several solutions for troubleshooting and resolving common problems. Whether it's your device freezing, Wi-Fi connection problems, or issues with sound, display, and performance, this guide will provide you with actionable steps to get your phone back to its optimal performance.

In this chapter, we will explore how to troubleshoot and resolve common problems with the Samsung Galaxy S25 Ultra, offering solutions for everything from device freezing to network connection issues. Let's dive into the solutions you can apply to keep your device running smoothly.

Device Not Responding: Quick Fixes

It's not uncommon for smartphones, including the Galaxy S25 Ultra, to occasionally freeze or become unresponsive.

This can be frustrating, but most of the time, the issue can be resolved quickly. Here's how you can handle a device that's not responding.

How to Restart Your Galaxy S25 Ultra When It Freezes

A simple restart can often resolve temporary glitches, unresponsive apps, and slow performance. Here's how you can restart your Galaxy S25 Ultra:

Soft Restart:

Step 1: Press and hold the power button and volume down button simultaneously for about 7-10 seconds.

Step 2: The phone will automatically restart. You'll see the Samsung logo, indicating that the phone is rebooting.

A soft restart is a quick fix for most problems and works by closing all running apps and refreshing the system. It doesn't affect your data or settings.

Hard Restart (if the phone is completely frozen):

If your phone is completely unresponsive and you can't restart it using the soft restart method, try the hard reset.

Step 1: Press and hold the power button and volume down button together for at least 10-15 seconds until the screen turns off.

Step 2: Release the buttons when the Samsung logo appears, and the phone will restart.

A hard reset is a more forceful method of restarting your device, and it is typically used when the phone is completely unresponsive or frozen on a screen.

Soft and Hard Resets: What's the Difference?

While both soft and hard resets can solve problems when the phone freezes or becomes unresponsive, it's important to understand the difference between the two:

Soft Reset: A soft reset is a simple restart that doesn't cause any data loss. It just reboots the device and is effective in resolving minor software glitches, frozen apps, or slow performance.

Hard Reset: A hard reset is a more forceful reboot. It's used when the phone is completely frozen and not responding to regular commands. A hard reset doesn't delete any data, but it forces the system to reboot and refresh itself.

Both methods can be helpful when dealing with unresponsive devices, but a soft reset is the go-to option in most situations, and it should be tried first.

Wi-Fi and Network Issues

One of the most common issues users experience is trouble with Wi-Fi or mobile network connectivity. Whether it's trouble connecting to a Wi-Fi network or issues with 5G or 4G LTE mobile data, there are several troubleshooting steps you can take to fix these problems.

Troubleshooting Common Wi-Fi Connection Problems

Wi-Fi issues are frustrating but usually solvable with a few steps. Here's how you can troubleshoot Wi-Fi connectivity problems on your Galaxy S25 Ultra:

Ensure Wi-Fi is Turned On:

Swipe down from the top of the screen to open the Quick Settings panel. Ensure that the Wi-Fi icon is turned on. If it's off, tap the icon to turn it on.

Reconnect to the Wi-Fi Network:

Go to Settings > Connections > Wi-Fi and select the network you want to connect to. If the connection fails, try tapping

Forget and then reconnect by entering the Wi-Fi password again.

Restart Your Router:

Sometimes, the issue may not be with your phone, but with your router. Unplug your router for about 10-15 seconds, then plug it back in. Wait for the router to reboot and reconnect your phone.

Check for Interference:

Wi-Fi performance can be impacted by interference from other devices or physical barriers. Ensure that you're close enough to the router and that there are minimal obstructions between your phone and the router.

Disable Smart Network Switch:

The Smart Network Switch feature automatically switches from Wi-Fi to mobile data when your Wi-Fi signal is weak. This can sometimes cause connectivity issues. To disable it:

Go to Settings > Connections > Wi-Fi > Advanced and toggle Smart Network Switch off.

Check for Software Updates:

Go to Settings > Software update > Download and install to ensure your phone is running the latest software. Sometimes, a new update includes bug fixes that improve Wi-Fi connectivity.

Fixing Mobile Data Issues and Resetting Network Settings

Mobile data problems can prevent you from using your phone for internet browsing, streaming, and communication. Here's how you can fix issues with mobile data on your Galaxy S25 Ultra:

Ensure Mobile Data is Turned On:

Open Quick Settings by swiping down from the top of the screen, then check that the Mobile Data icon is turned on. If not, tap the icon to enable it.

Check for Network Coverage:

Verify that your carrier offers good coverage in your area. If you're in an area with poor signal reception, try moving to a different location with better reception.

Turn Airplane Mode On and Off:

Sometimes toggling Airplane Mode can help reset your mobile data connection. To do this, swipe down from the top of the screen to open Quick Settings and tap the Airplane Mode icon. Wait for about 10 seconds, then turn it off.

Reset Network Settings:

If you're still facing issues, you may need to reset your network settings:

Go to Settings > General management > Reset > Reset network settings.

This will reset all your network settings, including Wi-Fi, mobile data, and Bluetooth, to their default values. After resetting, you'll need to reconnect to your Wi-Fi networks and re-pair your Bluetooth devices.

Check APN Settings:

If you're having issues with mobile data specifically, check the APN (Access Point Name) settings provided by your carrier. Go to Settings > Connections > Mobile networks > Access Point Names and ensure the settings match those provided by your carrier.

Sound, Display, and Performance Troubles

Sometimes, the Galaxy S25 Ultra may experience issues with sound, display, or overall performance. These issues can be related to software settings or hardware, but they can often be resolved by following a few troubleshooting steps.

Solving Sound Problems: No Sound or Low Volume Issues

Sound issues can prevent you from enjoying music, media, and phone calls. Here's how to fix common sound problems:

Check Volume Settings:

Make sure the volume is turned up. Press the volume buttons on the side of the device to increase the sound.

Check the Sound settings by going to Settings > Sounds and vibration, and ensure Media volume, Ringtone volume, and Notification volume are all appropriately set.

Check Do Not Disturb Mode:

Do Not Disturb mode can silence your phone's sound, including calls, notifications, and media. To turn it off, go to Settings > Sounds and vibration > Do Not Disturb and toggle it off.

Test with Headphones:

Plug in a pair of wired headphones or connect via Bluetooth to check if sound works through them. This can help determine if the problem is with the phone's speaker or audio output in general.

Check for Software Updates:

Sometimes, sound issues are due to a software bug. Check for updates by going to Settings > Software update > Download and install.

Test with Safe Mode:

Safe Mode can help you determine if third-party apps are causing sound issues. To enter Safe Mode:

Press and hold the power button.

Tap Power off, then press and hold it again until the Safe Mode prompt appears.

If sound works in Safe Mode, third-party apps are likely causing the issue. Try uninstalling recently installed apps.

Fixing Screen Responsiveness and Brightness Problems

The Galaxy S25 Ultra features a high-quality Dynamic AMOLED display that is designed to be responsive and bright. However, if the screen is unresponsive or the brightness is too low, here are steps to troubleshoot:

Check Touchscreen Responsiveness:

If the touchscreen is unresponsive or lagging, try restarting the device using the soft or hard reset methods described earlier. This can resolve issues with software or system glitches.

If the issue persists, check for screen protector interference. Some screen protectors may affect touchscreen sensitivity. Try removing it to see if the responsiveness improves.

Adjust Screen Brightness:

Go to Settings > Display > Brightness and adjust the slider to increase or decrease brightness. You can also enable Adaptive brightness to let the phone automatically adjust brightness based on ambient light.

Enable or Disable Adaptive Display:

The Adaptive Display feature optimizes color and contrast based on the content being viewed. If this causes issues, you can toggle it off in Settings > Display > Screen mode and select a different display mode.

Check for Software Updates:

Display-related problems can sometimes be resolved with a software update. Make sure your phone is up to date by going to Settings > Software update > Download and install.

Speed Up Performance by Managing Apps and Storage

As time goes on, your Galaxy S25 Ultra may slow down due to the accumulation of apps, cached data, and other temporary files. Here's how to speed up your phone:

Uninstall Unnecessary Apps:

Go to Settings > Apps and uninstall apps you no longer use. Removing unused apps will free up storage and system resources.

Clear Cache:

Cached data can slow down your device. To clear the cache, go to Settings > Storage > Cached data and tap Clear cached data. This will free up space without deleting any important data.

Use Device Care:

Go to Settings > Battery and device care > Optimize now. This tool scans for apps that are consuming excessive resources and optimizes the system to improve performance.

Factory Reset:

If your phone is still slow after cleaning up apps and data, a factory reset might be necessary. This will erase all data and return the device to its default settings. To do this, go to Settings > General management > Reset > Factory data reset.

The Samsung Galaxy S25 Ultra is a powerful device, but like any smartphone, it can occasionally experience issues. Whether it's freezing, Wi-Fi connectivity problems, sound issues, or sluggish performance, the solutions provided in this chapter will help you troubleshoot and resolve common problems.

By following the tips outlined here, you can keep your device running smoothly, resolve problems quickly, and ensure that you're always getting the best performance from your Galaxy S25 Ultra. Whether it's using a soft reset to unfreeze your phone, fixing connectivity issues, or optimizing performance, these troubleshooting techniques will help you maintain an optimal user experience.

CHAPTER 9

Getting the Most Out of Your Galaxy S25 Ultra

The Samsung Galaxy S25 Ultra is a powerhouse of features designed to enhance your mobile experience. With a sleek design, powerful hardware, and a suite of software tools, it offers everything you need to stay connected, productive, and entertained. However, to truly unlock the potential of your Galaxy S25 Ultra, it's important to dive deeper into its app ecosystem, services, and customization options. Whether you're looking to optimize your device with third-party apps, leverage Samsung's ecosystem, or discover hidden features, this guide will help you get the most out of your device.

In this chapter, we'll explore how to find useful apps, integrate with Samsung's services, and apply tips and tricks to enhance your overall experience.

Exploring the Galaxy Store and Third-Party Apps

The Galaxy S25 Ultra offers extensive customization options, especially through the Galaxy Store and third-party apps. The Galaxy Store provides a curated selection of apps and tools optimized for your Galaxy device. However, third-party apps from the Google Play Store also play a crucial role in extending your device's functionality. Let's explore how to discover useful apps, install them, and further personalize your Galaxy S25 Ultra with widgets and third-party tools.

Discovering Useful Apps and Games for Your Galaxy Device

The Galaxy Store features a range of apps, games, and content that are optimized for Samsung devices. Whether you're interested in productivity tools, social media apps, fitness trackers, or entertainment, there are plenty of apps to choose from.

Navigating the Galaxy Store:

Open the Galaxy Store app on your S25 Ultra by either tapping on the app icon in your app drawer or swiping up to search for it.

Browse through various categories, including Apps, Games, Themes, Watch faces, and more. You can also search directly for specific apps or games using the search bar at the top of the screen.

Popular Apps for Productivity and Utilities:

Samsung Notes: For quick note-taking, sketches, and saving ideas, Samsung Notes is an essential app that syncs with your Samsung account.

Samsung Health: Track your fitness goals and health metrics with Samsung Health, which provides detailed insights into your physical activity, heart rate, and sleep patterns.

Samsung Members: Use this app to access device diagnostics, get expert advice, and explore useful Samsung tips and tricks.

Games and Entertainment:

The Galaxy Store is home to a vast collection of mobile games, including both casual games and graphically demanding titles. Popular games like PUBG Mobile, Call of Duty Mobile, and Asphalt 9: Legends can be found here. Many of these games are optimized for the powerful hardware of the S25 Ultra, delivering smooth gameplay.

Installing Apps from the Google Play Store:

In addition to the Galaxy Store, the Google Play Store is another key resource for apps. Open the Play Store and browse categories such as Entertainment, Social, Productivity, Education, and Lifestyle.

Search for your preferred app or game, and simply tap Install to begin the download. After the app is installed, you can access it directly from your home screen or app drawer.

Optimizing Apps for Galaxy Devices:

Many apps in the Galaxy Store are optimized specifically for Samsung devices, offering features such as Samsung DeX support, edge panel integration, and S Pen compatibility (if applicable). This ensures that your apps provide the best possible experience on your Galaxy S25 Ultra.

Customizing Your Device Further with Widgets and Third-Party Tools

Widgets allow you to bring useful information and features directly to your home screen. Whether it's a weather widget, a calendar, or quick shortcuts to your favorite apps, widgets make your Galaxy S25 Ultra even more personalized.

Adding Widgets:

To add a widget, long-press an empty space on your home screen, and select Widgets. You'll be presented with a list of available widgets.

Choose a widget and drag it to your home screen. Resize it by dragging the corners to adjust its size.

Popular widgets include Clock, Weather, Samsung Calendar, and Bixby Routines. You can also add widgets for third-party apps like Spotify or YouTube.

Third-Party Customization Tools:

If you want more control over your home screen or other UI elements, consider third-party apps like Nova Launcher, Action Launcher, or Smart Launcher. These apps provide enhanced customization options for app layouts, icons, themes, and more.

Organizing Your Home Screen:

To keep your device organized, create folders for similar apps. Simply drag one app on top of another to create a folder, and name it according to its content (e.g., "Games," "Social," or "Finance").

Personalizing Your Themes and Icons:

The Galaxy Store offers themes and icon packs that allow you to change the look of your device. You can find these under Themes in the Galaxy Store. Select a theme or icon pack that suits your style, and apply it to your phone.

Additionally, you can change the font and system icons via Settings > Display > Screen mode to customize the look and feel.

Samsung Services: Exploring the Ecosystem

Samsung's ecosystem is designed to work seamlessly across multiple devices, offering a connected experience that makes managing your digital life easier. From Samsung Health for fitness tracking to Samsung Notes for note-taking, Samsung's services are deeply integrated into the Galaxy S25 Ultra. Furthermore, Samsung's ecosystem includes features like Bixby, Samsung DeX, and integrations with wearables like the Galaxy Watch. Let's explore these services in detail.

Understanding Samsung's Ecosystem: Samsung Health, Samsung Notes, and Bixby

Samsung Health:

Samsung Health is an essential app for monitoring your fitness and wellness. It tracks everything from steps and exercise to sleep patterns and heart rate. You can also set fitness goals and use it in conjunction with devices like the Galaxy Watch for real-time tracking.

Syncing with Wearables: To get the most out of Samsung Health, pair your Galaxy Watch with your S25 Ultra. This will provide even more detailed health data and fitness insights, such as workout tracking, GPS activity, and more.

Samsung Notes:

Samsung Notes is an intuitive app for note-taking and organizing thoughts. Whether you're jotting down a quick idea, creating checklists, or drawing sketches, Samsung Notes integrates seamlessly with the S Pen for precision note-taking.

Sync Across Devices: One of the best features of Samsung Notes is its ability to sync across all your Samsung devices, including tablets and PCs. This ensures you can access your notes anytime, anywhere.

Bixby:

Bixby is Samsung's voice assistant, and it's deeply integrated into the Galaxy S25 Ultra. You can use Bixby for a variety of tasks, including setting reminders, checking the weather, controlling smart home devices, sending messages, and more. Bixby offers hands-free convenience and can be activated by saying, "Hey, Bixby" or by pressing the Bixby button (if configured).

Bixby Routines: Bixby also allows you to create automated routines based on time, location, and app usage. For example, you can set up a routine to silence your phone during meetings or turn on Do Not Disturb when you're at the gym.

How to Integrate Your Galaxy S25 Ultra with Other Samsung Devices Like Tablets and Wearables

One of the key advantages of Samsung's ecosystem is how well the Galaxy S25 Ultra integrates with other Samsung devices, such as Galaxy Tab tablets, Galaxy Buds, Galaxy Watch, and more. This integration allows you to use your devices together to create a seamless and connected experience.

Pairing with Galaxy Wearables:

If you own a Galaxy Watch or Galaxy Buds, pairing them with your S25 Ultra is easy. For the Galaxy Watch, download the Samsung Galaxy Wearable app from the Google Play Store or Galaxy Store and follow the on-screen instructions to pair it with your phone.

The Galaxy Buds can also be connected via Bluetooth, and you'll be able to control music, take calls, and activate voice assistants directly from your earbuds.

Using Samsung DeX:

Samsung DeX is a feature that turns your Galaxy S25 Ultra into a desktop-like experience. Simply connect your phone to a monitor, keyboard, and mouse to use your phone as a full-fledged workstation. You can run apps in separate windows, manage documents, and multitask just like on a traditional computer.

Syncing with a Galaxy Tab:

Samsung's Galaxy Tab tablets can also work seamlessly with your S25 Ultra. You can use Samsung Flow to sync files, photos, and messages between your phone and tablet. This allows you to move content from your phone to your tablet with ease and vice versa.

SmartThings Integration:

The SmartThings app lets you control a wide range of Samsung and third-party smart devices from your phone, including lights, thermostats, security cameras, and more. This app brings all your smart devices into a unified ecosystem, allowing you to manage them from your Galaxy S25 Ultra.

Tips and Tricks to Enhance Your Experience

To maximize your Galaxy S25 Ultra experience, there are numerous tips and tricks you can use to make your device more efficient, personalized, and powerful. From voice commands to shortcut customization, here's how to enhance your phone's functionality.

Using Voice Commands with Bixby and Google Assistant

Voice assistants like Bixby and Google Assistant can save you time and make your phone experience more convenient. Here's how to use voice commands effectively:

Bixby Voice:

Activate Bixby Voice by saying "Hey Bixby" or holding the Bixby button. You can ask it to perform a variety of tasks, such as setting reminders, sending messages, controlling smart home devices, and opening apps.

Bixby Vision allows you to use your camera for live translations, shopping recommendations, and more.

Google Assistant:

Google Assistant is available on the Galaxy S25 Ultra as well. You can activate it by saying "Hey Google" or pressing the Home button (depending on settings). Google Assistant can perform many tasks, including controlling your music, providing weather updates, sending texts, and more.

Voice Commands for Hands-Free Use:

Both Bixby and Google Assistant allow you to control your device hands-free, making it easier to manage tasks while driving, cooking, or exercising. For example, you can ask Google Assistant to read your latest messages or ask Bixby to turn on your flashlight.

Customizing Shortcuts and Quick Actions for Efficiency

The Galaxy S25 Ultra allows you to streamline your phone's functionality by creating custom shortcuts and quick actions. These options can save you time and improve your overall efficiency.

Creating App Shortcuts:

You can create shortcuts for apps, settings, and specific actions directly on your home screen. Simply tap and hold an app icon and select Add shortcut or Create shortcut to place it on your home screen.

Quick Actions for Apps:

Some apps offer quick actions that allow you to perform common tasks directly from the home screen or app drawer.

For example, you can press and hold the Contacts app icon to quickly call or message a specific contact.

Edge Panels for Easy Access:

The Edge Panel feature gives you easy access to your favorite apps and tools from the edge of the screen. You can customize your Edge Panel to include apps, shortcuts, and even tools like Samsung Notes or Calculator.

Discovering Hidden Features in One UI

One UI, Samsung's custom skin on Android, is packed with hidden features and settings that can enhance your user experience. Here are some of the best hidden features to explore:

One-Handed Mode:

If you find the S25 Ultra's screen too large for one-handed use, you can enable One-handed Mode. To activate it, swipe down from the bottom corners of the screen, or go to Settings > Advanced features > One-handed mode.

App Lock:

For extra privacy, you can lock individual apps using App Lock. Go to Settings > Biometrics and security > App Lock, and set a PIN, password, or biometric lock for specific apps.

Digital Wellbeing:

Digital Wellbeing helps you manage your phone usage and reduce screen time. You can set app timers, enable Focus Mode, and track your device usage from Settings > Digital Wellbeing.

Edge Lighting:

For an exciting visual effect, enable Edge Lighting for incoming calls or notifications. You can customize the color and style by going to Settings > Display > Edge screen > Edge lighting.

The Samsung Galaxy S25 Ultra is a feature-packed device that offers endless opportunities for customization and productivity. Whether you're exploring the Galaxy Store for new apps, leveraging Samsung's ecosystem to sync your devices, or discovering hidden features in One UI, the Galaxy S25 Ultra is built to offer a personalized, efficient, and enjoyable mobile experience. By taking advantage of the tips and tricks outlined in this chapter, you can truly unlock the full potential of your Galaxy S25 Ultra, making it a device that works seamlessly for your unique needs and preferences.

CONCLUSION

Mastering the Samsung Galaxy S25 Ultra

As we reach the conclusion of our journey through the powerful features and functionalities of the Samsung Galaxy S25 Ultra, it's clear that this device represents the pinnacle of smartphone technology. With its stunning design, cutting-edge hardware, and unparalleled features, the Galaxy S25 Ultra sets new standards for what a smartphone can achieve. This device is not just a tool for communication and entertainment, but a comprehensive platform that empowers users to do more—whether that's through advanced photography, multi-tasking with Samsung DeX, or staying connected to the Samsung ecosystem of wearables and other smart devices.

Throughout this guide, we've explored the many facets of the Galaxy S25 Ultra, from its sleek, high-quality design to the versatile software tools and advanced customization options it offers. We've also dived deep into how to enhance your experience with this device, ensuring that you get the most out of its features, whether you're a professional, gamer, content creator, or casual user.

In this final chapter, let's take a moment to reflect on everything the Samsung Galaxy S25 Ultra brings to the table and how it can enhance your everyday life.

A Device Built for Performance and Style

One of the first things you'll notice about the Galaxy S25 Ultra is its sleek, futuristic design. With its Dynamic AMOLED display, the device offers one of the most stunning screens available on any smartphone today. Whether you're streaming your favorite content in 4K or playing a graphically intense game, the Galaxy S25 Ultra's 6.8-inch display provides an immersive experience that's second to none.

But beyond the visual appeal, the Galaxy S25 Ultra doesn't compromise when it comes to performance. Powered by the Snapdragon 8 Gen 2 or Exynos 2200 chipset (depending on your region), this phone is designed to handle everything from multitasking to gaming and creative applications with ease. Coupled with up to 12GB of RAM and 1TB of storage, you have ample power to store your apps, photos, and videos while running multiple programs simultaneously without lag.

What makes the Galaxy S25 Ultra stand out even further is its advanced camera system. With a 200MP main sensor and an array of telephoto, ultra-wide, and depth sensors, this phone brings professional-grade photography to your pocket. Whether you're shooting landscapes, portrait shots, or nighttime photography, the S25 Ultra's camera system gives you the flexibility to capture the world with incredible detail and accuracy. This is the phone that brings your photography ambitions to life.

Connecting You to the Future with 5G and Samsung's Ecosystem

As we move further into the future, 5G connectivity is going to play a significant role in how we interact with our smartphones and the world around us. The Samsung Galaxy S25 Ultra is ready for this change, equipped with 5G technology that allows you to enjoy ultra-fast internet speeds, faster downloads, and seamless streaming, all of which make your mobile experience even more efficient.

But the S25 Ultra doesn't just focus on speed and performance—it also seamlessly integrates with Samsung's ecosystem. Through Samsung DeX, you can transform your phone into a desktop-like experience, using your Galaxy S25 Ultra as a workstation on the go. For those who enjoy smart home technology, you can connect your device with Samsung SmartThings, and effortlessly manage and control a wide range of smart devices from your phone.

The integration doesn't stop at your phone either. If you have Samsung wearables like the Galaxy Watch, or use Galaxy Buds, the Galaxy S25 Ultra makes it easy to sync your data across all your Samsung devices, ensuring that everything from your fitness data to your entertainment preferences is always up to date.

Samsung's ecosystem is designed to offer a cohesive and intuitive user experience, allowing you to switch between devices effortlessly, whether you're using your phone to take a call or your tablet to browse the web.

Maximizing the User Experience with Advanced Features

In addition to its robust hardware and software integration, the Galaxy S25 Ultra comes with a wealth of advanced features designed to enhance the user experience:

S Pen Integration

The S Pen, exclusive to the S25 Ultra in the Galaxy S series, takes productivity and creativity to the next level. Whether you're taking notes, sketching, or controlling your device remotely with Air Actions, the S Pen offers unparalleled precision and convenience. With the ability to jot down notes without unlocking your phone through Screen Off Memo, and the versatility to create detailed drawings with Samsung Notes, the S Pen truly amplifies the capabilities of the S25 Ultra.

One UI and Customization

Samsung's One UI has evolved over the years into a sleek, feature-rich interface that provides a clean and user-friendly experience. With customizable themes, app shortcuts, and widgets, One UI gives you the flexibility to tailor your device to suit your personal preferences. Whether it's adjusting display settings for optimal eye comfort with Blue Light Filter or simplifying tasks with Bixby Routines, One UI offers something for everyone.

The ability to personalize your phone with widgets, icon packs, and wallpapers makes the S25 Ultra an extension of your personality and preferences. The device's Edge Panel feature allows quick access to your favorite apps and contacts, while Quick Actions streamline your phone's functions, saving you time and enhancing productivity.

Samsung Knox and Security Features

Security is paramount, and Samsung has equipped the S25 Ultra with Samsung Knox, a powerful defense system that protects both the software and hardware of your phone. From biometric authentication (fingerprint and facial recognition) to Secure Folder and Privacy Dashboard, the Galaxy S25 Ultra ensures that your personal information remains protected. This is especially crucial in an age where data privacy is more important than ever. With these robust security features, you can rest easy knowing that your sensitive information is in safe hands.

Battery Life and Power Management

Battery life is always a crucial consideration when it comes to smartphones, and the S25 Ultra delivers exceptional performance in this regard. With a 5000mAh battery and 45W fast charging capability, you'll be able to power through your day without worrying about running out of juice. For those moments when you need an extra boost, Wireless PowerShare allows you to charge other devices wirelessly using the phone's battery.

Moreover, adaptive battery settings and power-saving modes help you extend battery life when needed, ensuring that you can use your device for longer without needing to plug it in.

Samsung has also integrated 5G into the device, which brings faster data speeds while being energy efficient. This means you can enjoy blazing-fast internet without sacrificing battery life.

Versatility for Work, Play, and Creativity

The Samsung Galaxy S25 Ultra is not just a phone; it's a platform for creativity, work, and entertainment. With Samsung DeX, you can turn your phone into a full desktop experience, connecting it to external monitors, keyboards, and mice for an efficient workspace wherever you are. Whether you're working on documents, creating presentations, or browsing the web, DeX makes it easy to multitask on a larger screen.

For gamers, the S25 Ultra delivers top-notch performance, whether you're playing PUBG Mobile or Call of Duty Mobile. The Qualcomm Snapdragon 8 Gen 2 and 120Hz refresh rate display offer a buttery-smooth experience that rivals most gaming consoles, bringing your favorite titles to life.

On the creative front, the 200MP camera system provides incredible detail and flexibility, whether you're shooting professional-grade photos, recording in 8K video, or using Pro Mode to tweak every aspect of your shots. The S Pen takes your creativity even further, allowing you to sketch, write, and capture ideas effortlessly.

A Device for the Future

With the Samsung Galaxy S25 Ultra, you're not just purchasing a high-end smartphone; you're investing in the future of mobile technology. This device integrates the latest innovations, from 5G and AI-powered features to advanced photography and mobile desktop solutions like Samsung DeX. It's a phone that adapts to your needs, whether you're a creative professional, an executive, a gamer, or someone who simply wants a phone that performs well in every aspect of life.

As the world of mobile technology continues to evolve, the S25 Ultra stands as a testament to what's possible when innovation, design, and technology come together. Whether you're navigating your workday, capturing beautiful moments, or simply enjoying your favorite content, the Galaxy S25 Ultra ensures that you do so with ease, speed, and precision.

The Samsung Galaxy S25 Ultra is an all-in-one device that combines power, performance, and elegance. It offers unparalleled features that can cater to a wide variety of needs, from professional use to entertainment, gaming, and creativity. With its stunning design, cutting-edge technology, and seamless integration with the Samsung ecosystem, the Galaxy S25 Ultra is more than just a phone; it's an experience.

By now, you should have a deep understanding of everything the S25 Ultra has to offer, from its camera system and 5G connectivity to its productivity tools and customization options. This device is built to make your life easier, more efficient, and more enjoyable.

In the rapidly changing world of smartphones, the Galaxy S25 Ultra stands out as a device that sets a new benchmark for mobile excellence. Whether you're an avid tech enthusiast or someone looking for a reliable and powerful phone, the Galaxy S25 Ultra has everything you need to stay ahead of the curve. So, dive in, explore its features, and start getting the most out of your Samsung Galaxy S25 Ultra today.

www.ingramcontent.com/pod-product-compliance
Lightning Source LLC
Chambersburg PA
CBHW071254050326
40690CB00011B/2391